PHRIXUS AND HELLE

ÆSON AND JASON

CHIRON'S FAREWELL TO THE ARGONAUTS

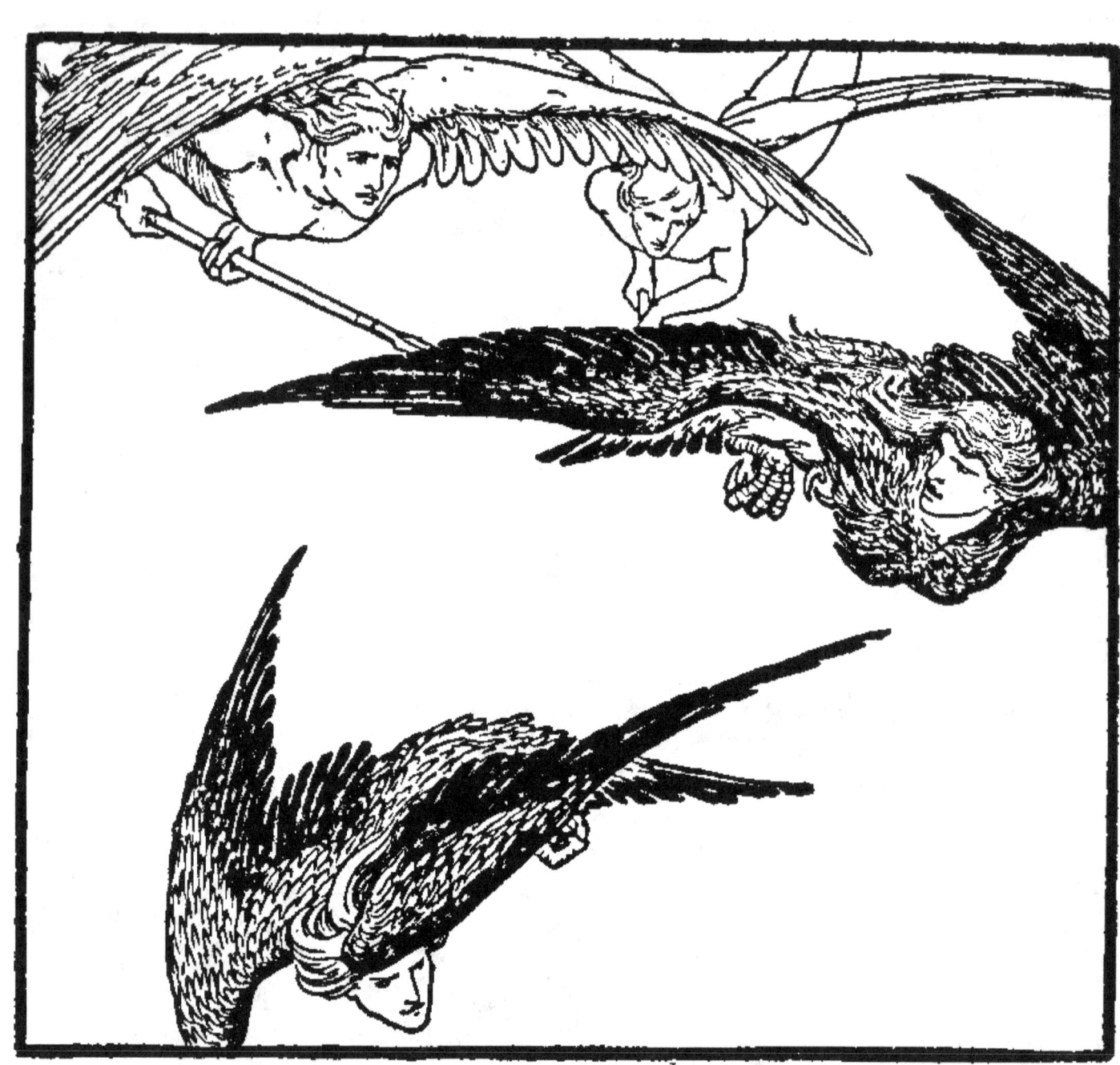

THE CHASE OF THE HARPIES

THE CROP OF THE DRAGON'S TEETH

ORPHEVS·AND·MEDEA·CHARM
THE·SNAKE·THAT·GVARDS·THE
GOLDEN·FLEECE·

CIRCE AND MEDEA

THE BEGUILING OF TALUS

THE GIANT ANTS

THE MONSTER OF THE FEATS

THE RED HOT SWINE

THE MILL OF GRUDGING

THE QUEEN OF THE MAGIC CLEW

THE GREAT BIRD

THE PERSIAN AND HASAN

THE PERSIAN SEWS UP HASAN

THE FLIGHT OF THE SWAN MAIDENS

HASAN'S WIFE CARRIES OFF HER CHILDREN

THE SHAYKH ABU AL-RUWAYSH

THE KING AND MANAR AL-SANA

HASAN REJOINS HIS WIFE

SHAWAHI ON THE JAR

THORKILL AND THE SERPENT

THE HORN-SNOUTED GIANTS

First edition, published in 2018 A Quick Guide to Time Management

William E. Cullen. B.Sc.

ISBN-13 978-1722014445

ISBN-10: 172201444X

Title ID: 8492798

BISAC Code: BUS 041000

Business & Economics – Management

Quick Time Management Skills Booklet

<u>Self Assessment</u>

Which practises works for me?

Which practise that I consider important, do I seldom act upon? Why?

Which three behaviours would give me most control over my life?	
New behaviour	**Desired result**
1.	
2.	
3.	

Identify your Energy Levels

- Identify your energy levels below, to map yourself, then try to plan your day to coincide with those various energy and task levels.
- For instance if you have a very important task at 11 am and your energy level then is high put a V at the intersection of 11 and High. And do the same for when your energy levels are lower, do the less important tasks then.
- You are in charge, and that is why the table covers all hours. After all you might be a night owl and full of energy when others sleep. But make sure though that *you* get sufficient rest time, to recharge your batteries.
- Reproduce the table below for at least a week or longer so you have an accurate view of how you are coping over that period.

What are your Energy Levels for tasks throughout a single day?

Energy level:	Morning						Afternoon						Evening						Night					
Tasks: V=Very Important I=Important R=Routine N=Not important L=Leisure / sleep																								
Time.	6	7	8	9	10	11	12	1	2	3	4	5	6	7	8	9	10	11	12	1	2	3	4	5
Very High.																								
High.																								
Medium.																								
Low.																								
Sleep.																								
Enter one of the task codes for each energy level.																								

Your Behaviour	Scoring Criteria 1: Seldom: 2: Sometimes: 3: Frequently:
1. I look back on my to-do list and find if I have accomplished the important tasks	1. – 2. – 3. –
2. Each member of my household has clearly defined household duties.	1. – 2. – 3. –
3. I am aware of my daily energy levels.	1. – 2. – 3. –
4. I am organised well enough to find an important letter in less than 5 minutes.	1. – 2. – 3. –
5. I ask for help when I want it.	1. – 2. – 3. –
6. I complete my most important tasks when I feel most energetic.	1. – 2. – 3. –
7. I delegate as many responsibilities as I can.	1. – 2. – 3. –
8. I have adequate time to be with friends and loved ones.	1. – 2. – 3. –
9. I make use of a daily planner or calendar to record important events and tasks.	1. – 2. – 3. –
10. I plan ahead by setting aside time on my calendar to complete major tasks.	1. – 2. – 3. –
11. I rank my priorities daily from most to least important.	1. – 2. – 3. –
12. I limit the amount of time each day that I devote to phone calls and emails.	1. – 2. – 3. –
13. I schedule time for interruptions.	1. – 2. – 3. –
14. I strive to handle each item in my mail only once.	1. – 2. – 3. –
15. I take good care of myself by rewarding myself at least twice a week.	1. – 2. – 3. –
16. I take good care of myself by rewarding myself for completing realistic objectives.	1. – 2. – 3. –
17. I use a "to do" list daily.	1. – 2. – 3. –
18. I work on my most important tasks before I work on the easy ones.	1. – 2. – 3. –
19. When I face an unpleasant task, I break the task into bite sized pieces.	1. – 2. – 3. –
20. When necessary I set limits by saying "No I just don't have enough time right now for that".	1. – 2. – 3. –
Total (between 20 and 60)	__

	What five things do you want to change? Lifetime goals / dreams etc.:
1	
2.	
3.	
4.	
5.	

	Five goals to be achieved within 5 years?
1.	
2.	
3.	
4.	
5.	

	Your single most important 5 year goal, if you only had 6 months to live?
Goal:	

	List and rank the five steps you will take in the next 6 months to achieve this goal.	
	Steps:	Order
1.		—
2.		—
3.		—
4.		—
5.		—

Keeping a time log

Time log activity codes

Code	Activity code:	
1.	Conferences.	• Analyse at what times you were most productive, what tasks took the most time, and what they were (e.g. work, family, personal, recreation).
2.	Eating / Drinking.	
3.	Emails / Telephone.	
4.	Holiday.	• Are you devoting most of your time to the most important items?
5.	Meetings.	• Do some tasks require better time planning than others?
6.	Recreation.	
7.	Sleep / Rest.	• Evaluate whether you did what you wanted to do or not in that time.
8.	Travel to / from work.	
9.	Work alone.	• Keep a log for a week or more, detailing what you are doing every hour.
10.	[You to decide].	

Enter below, the relevant activity code number from above, for each time slot.

Day	Mon.	Tues.	Wed.	Thurs.	Fri.	Sat.	Sun.
Time:	Activity Code						
0600	–	–	–	–	–	–	–
0700	–	–	–	–	–	–	–
0800	–	–	–	–	–	–	–
0900	–	–	–	–	–	–	–
1000	–	–	–	–	–	–	–
1100	–	–	–	–	–	–	–
1200	–	–	–	–	–	–	–
1300	–	–	–	–	–	–	–
1400	–	–	–	–	–	–	–
1500	–	–	–	–	–	–	–
1600	–	–	–	–	–	–	–
1700	–	–	–	–	–	–	–
1800	–	–	–	–	–	–	–
1900	–	–	–	–	–	–	–
2000	–	–	–	–	–	–	–
2100	–	–	–	–	–	–	–
2200	–	–	–	–	–	–	–
2300-0500	–	–	–	–	–	–	–

Set priorities:

- Create your to do list (daily / weekly / monthly / yearly / project).
- Re-rank your to-do list. A grid or two might help.
- What task or tasks are important, or urgent, or the most difficult to do?

Work priority

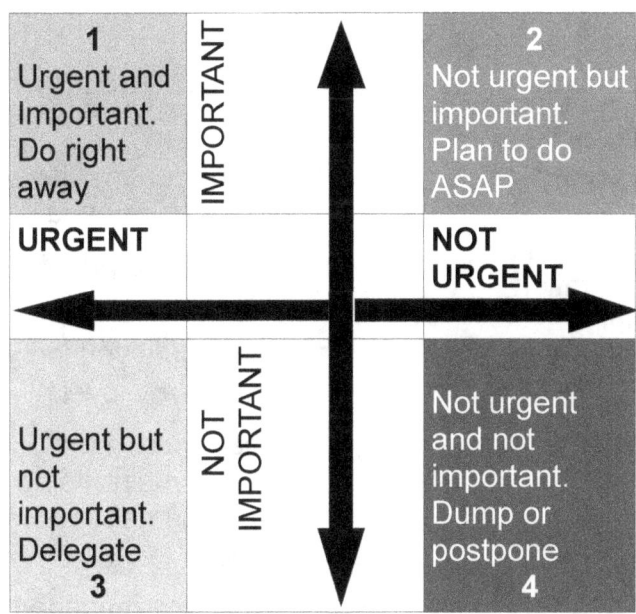

Project Priority

High		
Importance (e.g. Revenue Costs, Savings, Risks or not doing etc.)	**Quick wins**	**More Strategic (simplify or split)**
	Possibly re-consider?	**Drop?**
Low	**Difficulty (e.g. time, cost, effort, risk of complexity etc.)**	**High**

What are the characteristics of effective time management?:

- Prioritising, setting boundaries, and identifying current time management habits.

- Apply the benefits of effective time management in the professional realm?

	URGENT	NOT URGENT
IMPORTANT	1 Crises, Pressing Problems, Deadline Driven, Projects, Meetings, Preparations.	2 Preparations, Presentation Planning, Relationships Recreations,
NOT IMPORTANT	3 Interruptions, Some phone calls, Some mail, some reports, some meetings, Some pressing matters.	4 Trivia, Junk mail, Some phone calls, Time wasters, Escape activities, Games

Discussion questions:

- Do your energy levels play a part or hinder you in this?

- How do you prioritise your day?

- How would you log your time and energy levels?

- What are some of the ways to ensure you're doing what you want and need at work, and at home.

- What time management skills do you already practice?

Use planning tools

There are various types available:

- Filofaxes (nicely 80's).
- Paper.
- Planners / wall charts / index cards.
- Phone Apps.
  - to-do lists.
  - voice recorders.
  - calendars.
  - diaries.

Get organised

De-clutter your desk and sort it into three sections or trays labelled:

1. **Keep:**
   - Act on it then move it to one of the other two trays.
   - File it permanently.
   - File it temporarily then act on it when more information becomes known or it is time to act upon it.

2. **Give it away:**
   - Act on it then get rid of it.
   - Delegate someone to deal with it.

3. **Get rid of it:**
   - Lose these items immediately into the waste basket.

Schedule your time

- Block out time from interruptions, for highest priority tasks first.
- For waiting time / commuting – schedule small tasks.
- Knowing your energy levels, plan your hardest tasks for when your levels are highest.
- Use a suitable phone app (google calendar).
- You need the other ¼ for creative time / planning / thinking / reading.
- Your schedule is not just about what you have to do (meetings and appointments) but what you want to do – limit time to about ¾ of your day.

Get on with it and stop prevaricating

- Break these jobs down into manageable tasks, each of which can be done in short bursts of time.
- Build in a reward system to your tasks, when completed.
- Difficult jobs?
- Do you need to complete a preparatory task first?
- Keep putting these off – stop procrastinating?

Manage time wasters

Telephone:

- Do necessary actions immediately.
- Stand up when on the phone.
- Use voice mail setting aside time to return calls.
- Set aside time during the day to receive and not receive calls.

Visitors:

- Establish time blocks when you are available for visitors.
- If someone is at your door, meet standing up.
- Re-schedule unexpected visitors.

Meetings:

- Arrive on time knowing what the meeting is going to be about (find out).
- End on time.
- Only attend / set necessary meetings, advise chair of your absence and why.
- Prepare and use an agenda (timed agenda if necessary).

Mail and email:

- Answer written messages by using the margins etc.
- Don't let them accumulate before dealing with them.
- Handle each item only once.
- Set aside blocks of time to read and respond to mail and emails but:
  - sort mail near your waste bin and delete junk emails immediately.

Family obligations:

- Establish a master calendar to post family commitments onto.
- Tell your family to consult this and advise of conflicts.
- Use the fridge or somewhere where you can leave messages that. your family know how to find.

Avoid multitasking:

- Research shows this is not a productive use of your time.

Stay healthy:

- Reward yourself for time management successes.
- Schedule time off.
- Use your time according to your biological clock (when your energy log says is optimum) to do priority tasks and when you can concentrate the best.

What are your Energy Levels for tasks throughout a single day?

Energy level:	Morning						Afternoon						Evening						Night					
Tasks: V=Very Important I=Important R=Routine N=Not important L=Leisure / sleep																								
Time.	6	7	8	9	10	11	12	1	2	3	4	5	6	7	8	9	10	11	12	1	2	3	4	5
Very High.																								
High.																								
Medium.																								
Low.																								
Sleep.																								

Enter one of the task codes for each energy level.

What are your Energy Levels for tasks throughout a single day?

Energy level:	Morning						Afternoon						Evening						Night					
Tasks: V=Very Important I=Important R=Routine N=Not important L=Leisure / sleep																								
Time.	6	7	8	9	10	11	12	1	2	3	4	5	6	7	8	9	10	11	12	1	2	3	4	5
Very High.																								
High.																								
Medium.																								
Low.																								
Sleep.																								

Enter one of the task codes for each energy level.

What are your Energy Levels for tasks throughout a single day?

Energy level:	Morning						Afternoon						Evening						Night					
Tasks: V=Very Important I=Important R=Routine N=Not important L=Leisure / sleep																								
Time.	6	7	8	9	10	11	12	1	2	3	4	5	6	7	8	9	10	11	12	1	2	3	4	5
Very High.																								
High.																								
Medium.																								
Low.																								
Sleep.																								

Enter one of the task codes for each energy level.

What are your Energy Levels for tasks throughout a single day?

Energy level:	Morning						Afternoon						Evening						Night					
Tasks: V=Very Important I=Important R=Routine N=Not important L=Leisure / sleep																								
Time.	6	7	8	9	10	11	12	1	2	3	4	5	6	7	8	9	10	11	12	1	2	3	4	5
Very High.																								
High.																								
Medium.																								
Low.																								
Sleep.																								

Enter one of the task codes for each energy level.

What are your Energy Levels for tasks throughout a single day?

Energy level:	Morning						Afternoon						Evening						Night					
Tasks: V=Very Important I=Important R=Routine N=Not important L=Leisure / sleep																								
Time.	6	7	8	9	10	11	12	1	2	3	4	5	6	7	8	9	10	11	12	1	2	3	4	5
Very High.																								
High.																								
Medium.																								
Low.																								
Sleep.																								

Enter one of the task codes for each energy level.

What are your Energy Levels for tasks throughout a single day?

Energy level:	Morning						Afternoon						Evening						Night					
Tasks: V=Very Important I=Important R=Routine N=Not important L=Leisure / sleep																								
Time.	6	7	8	9	10	11	12	1	2	3	4	5	6	7	8	9	10	11	12	1	2	3	4	5
Very High.																								
High.																								
Medium.																								
Low.																								
Sleep.																								

Enter one of the task codes for each energy level.

What are your Energy Levels for tasks throughout a single day?

Energy level:	Morning						Afternoon						Evening						Night					
Tasks: V=Very Important I=Important R=Routine N=Not important L=Leisure / sleep																								
Time.	6	7	8	9	10	11	12	1	2	3	4	5	6	7	8	9	10	11	12	1	2	3	4	5
Very High.																								
High.																								
Medium.																								
Low.																								
Sleep.																								

Enter one of the task codes for each energy level.

What are your Energy Levels for tasks throughout a single day?

Energy level:	Morning						Afternoon						Evening						Night					
Tasks: V=Very Important I=Important R=Routine N=Not important L=Leisure / sleep																								
Time.	6	7	8	9	10	11	12	1	2	3	4	5	6	7	8	9	10	11	12	1	2	3	4	5
Very High.																								
High.																								
Medium.																								
Low.																								
Sleep.																								

Enter one of the task codes for each energy level.

What are your Energy Levels for tasks throughout a single day?

Energy level:	Morning						Afternoon						Evening						Night					
Tasks: V=Very Important I=Important R=Routine N=Not important L=Leisure / sleep																								
Time.	6	7	8	9	10	11	12	1	2	3	4	5	6	7	8	9	10	11	12	1	2	3	4	5
Very High.																								
High.																								
Medium.																								
Low.																								
Sleep.																								

Enter one of the task codes for each energy level.

What are your Energy Levels for tasks throughout a single day?

Energy level:	Morning							Afternoon						Evening						Night					
Tasks: V=Very Important I=Important R=Routine N=Not important L=Leisure / sleep																									
Time.	6	7	8	9	10	11	12	1	2	3	4	5	6	7	8	9	10	11	12	1	2	3	4	5
Very High.																								
High.																								
Medium.																								
Low.																								
Sleep.																								

Enter one of the task codes for each energy level.

What are your Energy Levels for tasks throughout a single day?

Energy level:	Morning							Afternoon						Evening						Night					
Tasks: V=Very Important I=Important R=Routine N=Not important L=Leisure / sleep																									
Time.	6	7	8	9	10	11	12	1	2	3	4	5	6	7	8	9	10	11	12	1	2	3	4	5
Very High.																								
High.																								
Medium.																								
Low.																								
Sleep.																								

Enter one of the task codes for each energy level.

What are your Energy Levels for tasks throughout a single day?

Energy level:	Morning							Afternoon						Evening						Night					
Tasks: V=Very Important I=Important R=Routine N=Not important L=Leisure / sleep																									
Time.	6	7	8	9	10	11	12	1	2	3	4	5	6	7	8	9	10	11	12	1	2	3	4	5
Very High.																								
High.																								
Medium.																								
Low.																								
Sleep.																								

Enter one of the task codes for each energy level.

What are your Energy Levels for tasks throughout a single day?

Energy level:	Morning						Afternoon						Evening						Night					

Tasks: V=Very Important I=Important R=Routine N=Not important L=Leisure / sleep

Time.	6	7	8	9	10	11	12	1	2	3	4	5	6	7	8	9	10	11	12	1	2	3	4	5
Very High.																								
High.																								
Medium.																								
Low.																								
Sleep.																								

Enter one of the task codes for each energy level.

What are your Energy Levels for tasks throughout a single day?

Energy level:	Morning						Afternoon						Evening						Night					

Tasks: V=Very Important I=Important R=Routine N=Not important L=Leisure / sleep

Time.	6	7	8	9	10	11	12	1	2	3	4	5	6	7	8	9	10	11	12	1	2	3	4	5
Very High.																								
High.																								
Medium.																								
Low.																								
Sleep.																								

Enter one of the task codes for each energy level.

What are your Energy Levels for tasks throughout a single day?

Energy level:	Morning						Afternoon						Evening						Night					

Tasks: V=Very Important I=Important R=Routine N=Not important L=Leisure / sleep

Time.	6	7	8	9	10	11	12	1	2	3	4	5	6	7	8	9	10	11	12	1	2	3	4	5
Very High.																								
High.																								
Medium.																								
Low.																								
Sleep.																								

Enter one of the task codes for each energy level.

Time log activity codes

Code	Activity code:
1.	Conferences.
2.	Eating / Drinking.
3.	Emails / Telephone.
4.	Holiday.
5.	Meetings.
6.	Recreation.
7.	Sleep / Rest.
8.	Travel to / from work.
9.	Work alone.
10.	[You to decide].

- Analyse at what times you were most productive, what tasks took the most time, and what they were (e.g. work, family, personal, recreation).
- Are you devoting most of your time to the most important items?
- Do some tasks require better time planning than others?
- Evaluate whether you did what you wanted to do or not in that time.
- Keep a log for a week or more, detailing what you are doing every hour.

Enter below, the relevant activity code number from above, for each time slot.

Day	Mon.	Tues.	Wed.	Thurs.	Fri.	Sat.	Sun.
Time:	Activity Code						
0600	–	–	–	–	–	–	–
0700	–	–	–	–	–	–	–
0800	–	–	–	–	–	–	–
0900	–	–	–	–	–	–	–
1000	–	–	–	–	–	–	–
1100	–	–	–	–	–	–	–
1200	–	–	–	–	–	–	–
1300	–	–	–	–	–	–	–
1400	–	–	–	–	–	–	–
1500	–	–	–	–	–	–	–
1600	–	–	–	–	–	–	–
1700	–	–	–	–	–	–	–
1800	–	–	–	–	–	–	–
1900	–	–	–	–	–	–	–
2000	–	–	–	–	–	–	–
2100	–	–	–	–	–	–	–
2200	–	–	–	–	–	–	–
2300-0500	–	–	–	–	–	–	–

Day	Mon.	Tues.	Wed.	Thurs.	Fri.	Sat.	Sun.
Enter below, the relevant activity code number from above, for each time slot.							
Time:	Activity Code						
0600	–	–	–	–	–	–	–
0700	–	–	–	–	–	–	–
0800	–	–	–	–	–	–	–
0900	–	–	–	–	–	–	–
1000	–	–	–	–	–	–	–
1100	–	–	–	–	–	–	–
1200	–	–	–	–	–	–	–
1300	–	–	–	–	–	–	–
1400	–	–	–	–	–	–	–
1500	–	–	–	–	–	–	–
1600	–	–	–	–	–	–	–
1700	–	–	–	–	–	–	–
1800	–	–	–	–	–	–	–
1900	–	–	–	–	–	–	–
2000	–	–	–	–	–	–	–
2100	–	–	–	–	–	–	–
2200	–	–	–	–	–	–	–
2300-0500	–	–	–	–	–	–	–

Day	Mon.	Tues.	Wed.	Thurs.	Fri.	Sat.	Sun.
Time:	**Activity Code**						
0600	–	–	–	–	–	–	–
0700	–	–	–	–	–	–	–
0800	–	–	–	–	–	–	–
0900	–	–	–	–	–	–	–
1000	–	–	–	–	–	–	–
1100	–	–	–	–	–	–	–
1200	–	–	–	–	–	–	–
1300	–	–	–	–	–	–	–
1400	–	–	–	–	–	–	–
1500	–	–	–	–	–	–	–
1600	–	–	–	–	–	–	–
1700	–	–	–	–	–	–	–
1800	–	–	–	–	–	–	–
1900	–	–	–	–	–	–	–
2000	–	–	–	–	–	–	–
2100	–	–	–	–	–	–	–
2200	–	–	–	–	–	–	–
2300-0500	–	–	–	–	–	–	–

Day	Mon.	Tues.	Wed.	Thurs.	Fri.	Sat.	Sun.
Time:	Activity Code						
0600	–	–	–	–	–	–	–
0700	–	–	–	–	–	–	–
0800	–	–	–	–	–	–	–
0900	–	–	–	–	–	–	–
1000	–	–	–	–	–	–	–
1100	–	–	–	–	–	–	–
1200	–	–	–	–	–	–	–
1300	–	–	–	–	–	–	–
1400	–	–	–	–	–	–	–
1500	–	–	–	–	–	–	–
1600	–	–	–	–	–	–	–
1700	–	–	–	–	–	–	–
1800	–	–	–	–	–	–	–
1900	–	–	–	–	–	–	–
2000	–	–	–	–	–	–	–
2100	–	–	–	–	–	–	–
2200	–	–	–	–	–	–	–
2300-0500	–	–	–	–	–	–	–

Enter below, the relevant activity code number from above, for each time slot.

Day	Mon.	Tues.	Wed.	Thurs.	Fri.	Sat.	Sun.
Time:	Activity Code						
0600	–	–	–	–	–	–	–
0700	–	–	–	–	–	–	–
0800	–	–	–	–	–	–	–
0900	–	–	–	–	–	–	–
1000	–	–	–	–	–	–	–
1100	–	–	–	–	–	–	–
1200	–	–	–	–	–	–	–
1300	–	–	–	–	–	–	–
1400	–	–	–	–	–	–	–
1500	–	–	–	–	–	–	–
1600	–	–	–	–	–	–	–
1700	–	–	–	–	–	–	–
1800	–	–	–	–	–	–	–
1900	–	–	–	–	–	–	–
2000	–	–	–	–	–	–	–
2100	–	–	–	–	–	–	–
2200	–	–	–	–	–	–	–
2300-0500	–	–	–	–	–	–	–

Enter below, the relevant activity code number from above, for each time slot.

Day	Mon.	Tues.	Wed.	Thurs.	Fri.	Sat.	Sun.
Time:	Activity Code						
0600	–	–	–	–	–	–	–
0700	–	–	–	–	–	–	–
0800	–	–	–	–	–	–	–
0900	–	–	–	–	–	–	–
1000	–	–	–	–	–	–	–
1100	–	–	–	–	–	–	–
1200	–	–	–	–	–	–	–
1300	–	–	–	–	–	–	–
1400	–	–	–	–	–	–	–
1500	–	–	–	–	–	–	–
1600	–	–	–	–	–	–	–
1700	–	–	–	–	–	–	–
1800	–	–	–	–	–	–	–
1900	–	–	–	–	–	–	–
2000	–	–	–	–	–	–	–
2100	–	–	–	–	–	–	–
2200	–	–	–	–	–	–	–
2300-0500	–	–	–	–	–	–	–

Enter below, the relevant activity code number from above, for each time slot.

Day	Mon.	Tues.	Wed.	Thurs.	Fri.	Sat.	Sun.
Time:	Activity Code						
0600	–	–	–	–	–	–	–
0700	–	–	–	–	–	–	–
0800	–	–	–	–	–	–	–
0900	–	–	–	–	–	–	–
1000	–	–	–	–	–	–	–
1100	–	–	–	–	–	–	–
1200	–	–	–	–	–	–	–
1300	–	–	–	–	–	–	–
1400	–	–	–	–	–	–	–
1500	–	–	–	–	–	–	–
1600	–	–	–	–	–	–	–
1700	–	–	–	–	–	–	–
1800	–	–	–	–	–	–	–
1900	–	–	–	–	–	–	–
2000	–	–	–	–	–	–	–
2100	–	–	–	–	–	–	–
2200	–	–	–	–	–	–	–
2300-0500	–	–	–	–	–	–	–

Enter below, the relevant activity code number from above, for each time slot.

Day	Mon.	Tues.	Wed.	Thurs.	Fri.	Sat.	Sun.
Enter below, the relevant activity code number from above, for each time slot.							
Time:	Activity Code						
0600	–	–	–	–	–	–	–
0700	–	–	–	–	–	–	–
0800	–	–	–	–	–	–	–
0900	–	–	–	–	–	–	–
1000	–	–	–	–	–	–	–
1100	–	–	–	–	–	–	–
1200	–	–	–	–	–	–	–
1300	–	–	–	–	–	–	–
1400	–	–	–	–	–	–	–
1500	–	–	–	–	–	–	–
1600	–	–	–	–	–	–	–
1700	–	–	–	–	–	–	–
1800	–	–	–	–	–	–	–
1900	–	–	–	–	–	–	–
2000	–	–	–	–	–	–	–
2100	–	–	–	–	–	–	–
2200	–	–	–	–	–	–	–
2300-0500	–	–	–	–	–	–	–

Day	Mon.	Tues.	Wed.	Thurs.	Fri.	Sat.	Sun.
Time:	**Activity Code**						
0600	–	–	–	–	–	–	–
0700	–	–	–	–	–	–	–
0800	–	–	–	–	–	–	–
0900	–	–	–	–	–	–	–
1000	–	–	–	–	–	–	–
1100	–	–	–	–	–	–	–
1200	–	–	–	–	–	–	–
1300	–	–	–	–	–	–	–
1400	–	–	–	–	–	–	–
1500	–	–	–	–	–	–	–
1600	–	–	–	–	–	–	–
1700	–	–	–	–	–	–	–
1800	–	–	–	–	–	–	–
1900	–	–	–	–	–	–	–
2000	–	–	–	–	–	–	–
2100	–	–	–	–	–	–	–
2200	–	–	–	–	–	–	–
2300-0500	–	–	–	–	–	–	–

Enter below, the relevant activity code number from above, for each time slot.